The ADVENT WREATH

A Light in the Darkness

by Debbie Trafton O'Neal

Augsburg Publishing House, Minneapolis

THE
ADVENT
WREATH

The word *advent* means "coming." Christians know and celebrate the season of Advent as a time of preparation and reflection in anticipation of Christmas, the celebration of Christ's birth. Throughout the Advent season, Christians also acknowledge and anticipate the promised second coming of Jesus Christ.

The History of Advent

Before the formation of the Christian church, Jewish custom dictated the celebration of the new year in the spring. At first, as the followers of Jesus began meeting together, they continued in this Jewish tradition.

There are indications, however, that Christians from year to year, even from century to century, eventually developed the rites and traditions of Christmas and the new year as a midwinter celebration. Midwinter, the time of the winter solstice when the sun is at its lowest ebb, has long been an important season for people of Northern cultures. It is the time of shortest daylight, when people yearn for the sun to return with its brightness and warmth, and look for a sign that spring will come.

By the fourth or fifth century, Christmas was established as a religious festival that signified the beginning of the ecclesiastical year. It was at this time that those in the Christian church celebrated the birth of God's Son, Jesus Christ, and after that the beginning of a new year.

In the year 529, Emperor Justinian also declared December 25 a civic holiday, an action that prohibited any work to be done on that day. Then in the year 567, the Council of Tours established the season of Advent as a time of fasting preceding Christmas Day. The council also proclaimed the 12 days from Christmas to Epiphany as a sacred season. At that time a period of fasting was maintained by those wishing to become a part of the Christian fellowship on the day of Epiphany, January 6.

Initially, the Advent period varied from three to seven weeks. Later it became customary to observe the season for four weeks.

4

This then became the actual beginning of the church year. Today we still look to Advent as the beginning of the church year. Although the dates change from year to year, Advent begins on the Sunday nearest to November 30 and contains the four Sundays before Christmas Day. The season can range anywhere from 23 to 28 days, depending on which day Christmas Eve falls.

Much like the season of Lent, Advent is thought of as a time of penitence and preparation for the coming of the King. As we ponder and anticipate the festival of Christmas, we can think of this coming in three ways:

1 The season of Advent represents the coming of the King as a human child. In the form of a baby, wrapped in cloth and laid to rest in a manger of straw, Jesus came to us. We commemorate this event on Christmas Day.

2 The season of Advent fills us with the coming of the King in Word and Spirit, about which we witness and for which we live the year around.

3 The season of Advent invites us to reflect on the second coming of the King—that time when Jesus will return in glory at the end of time as we know it.

The Advent Wreath

Shape

The origins of the Advent wreath are somewhat obscure. But it is thought that the first Advent wreath originated in Germany or France within the tradition of the Lutheran church. The sense of joyous anticipation that fills the Advent season has helped to popularize the Advent wreath, making it a part of all cultures and ethnic backgrounds.

The original wreath, a circle of wire, represented the unending love of God. Evergreens adorning the wreath symbolized the hope of eternal life that God's people share. Four candles set in the wreath represented the four weeks until Christmas Day, as well as the thousands of years people awaited the coming of the Messiah. The lighting of an additional candle each week in Advent marked the growing anticipation for the Light who came into the world at Jesus' birth.

Today's Advent wreaths take many forms, from simple wire circles adorned with evergreen branches to ceramic, metal, or carved-wood bases, some with evergreens and some without. Although the nature of a wreath is to be hung, this is not practical in many homes. So the Advent wreath is usually set on a table.

Color

In the early church, white was used as the liturgical color throughout the year. Not until the twelfth century do we find a reference to use of color in church tradition. At that time the color red was first used to represent Pentecost. Eventually, colors were assigned to the various seasons of the church year. The color of purple was chosen for both Advent and Lent. Paraments, altar cloths, and stoles used during these seasons have traditionally been purple. The rich color of purple suggests royalty, for we await a King.

In recent years, however, royal blue has become the preferred color to be used throughout the season of Advent. Blue not only distinguishes Advent from Lent, but also represents hope, a primary theme of the weeks before the festival we celebrate on Christmas Day.

These traditional uses of color offer guidelines for the color of candles used in the Advent wreath. Traditionally four candles are used, representing the four Sundays of the season. Purple candles are often used for the First, Second, and Fourth Sundays in Advent, and a pink or rose candle used on the Third Sunday in Advent. This different colored candle represents joy. It would be appropriate to substitute blue candles for the purple in an Advent wreath, either with or without the use of a pink candle on the third Sunday. Some people prefer to use all white candles in their Advent wreath. Or, as the season of Advent comes to an end, the four candles in the wreath might be replaced with fresh white ones on Christmas Eve. This can represent Jesus' birth bringing light into the world.

Candles

There is no historical tradition regarding the meaning of the candles used in the Advent wreath other than their marking the four weeks of Advent. Various explanations or designations for each of the four candles have sprung up, however. The most common themes are listed below:

First Candle. The coming of Jesus. As we light the first candle in the Advent wreath, we reflect on the birth and Parousia, or second coming, of Jesus.

Second Candle. The coming of Jesus. As with the first candle, our thoughts focus on the birth and second coming of Jesus.

Third Candle. John the Baptist—herald of Christ. With the lighting of the candle in the third week of Advent our thoughts turn to John the Baptist, the one who prepared the way for Christ.

6

Fourth Candle. Mary—God's obedient servant. In the fourth week of Advent, our thoughts turn to Mary, the obedient servant chosen by God to bear the Son in human form.

Each week as the appropriate candle is lit, a corresponding scripture is read that reflects the themes listed above.

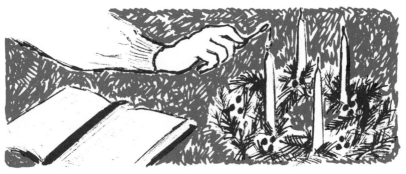

Planning a Home Celebration

For Advent to have its fullest impact, Christmas decorations, music, and parties might be delayed until the 12 days of Christmas—December 24 through January 5. Make the season of Advent a meaningful time in your home, using some of the ideas that follow.

● Purchase or make an Advent wreath, using one of the ideas found on pages 13-15.

● Make plans to gather around the Advent wreath weekly, if not daily, for a time to reflect upon the gift of love God shared with all people.

● In a family setting, decide together what kinds of things your time around the Advent wreath will include. Decide on a time (such as morning, evening, or mealtime) to meet. Talk about who will light or snuff out the candles.

● Choose appropriate scripture passages to read, either individually or with one person reading aloud. After the reading each day, take time to think about or discuss the passage, as well as any feelings or experiences that relate to the scripture reading.

● Sing or read aloud the words to an Advent hymn and reflect upon the significance those words have for your life.

In whatever way you choose to use your Advent wreath as the focus of your anticipation of Christmas, it will enrich the season for you.

Suggested Daily Bible Readings

Week One

Sunday	Matthew 25:1-13
Monday	Luke 20:1-8
Tuesday	Luke 20:9-18
Wednesday	Luke 20:19-26
Thursday	Luke 20:27-40
Friday	Luke 20:41—21:4
Saturday	Luke 21:5-19

Week Two

Sunday	Luke 7:28-35
Monday	Luke 21:20-28
Tuesday	Luke 21:29-38
Wednesday	John 7:53—8:11
Thursday	Luke 22:1-13
Friday	Luke 22:14-30
Saturday	Luke 22:31-38

Week Three

Sunday	John 3:22-30
Monday	Luke 22:39-53
Tuesday	Luke 22:54-69
Wednesday	Mark 1:1-8
Thursday	Matthew 3:1-12
Friday	Matthew 11:2-15
Saturday	Luke 3:1-9

Week Four

Sunday	John 3:16-21
Monday	John 5:30-47
Tuesday	Luke 1:5-25
Wednesday	Luke 1:26-38
Thursday	Luke 1:39-48a or Luke 1:48b-56
Friday	Luke 1:57-66
Saturday	Luke 1:67-80

Suggested Hymns

Come, thou long-expected Jesus

1 Come, thou long - ex - pect - ed Je - sus, Born to set thy peo - ple free;
2 Born thy peo - ple to de - liv - er, Born a child, and yet a king;

From our fears and sins re - lease us; Let us find our rest in thee.
Born to reign in us for - ev - er, Now thy gra - cious king - dom bring.

Is - rael's strength and con - so - la - tion, Hope of all the earth thou art,
By thine own e - ter - nal Spir - it Rule in all our hearts a - lone;

Dear de - sire of ev - 'ry na - tion, Joy of ev - 'ry long - ing heart.
By thine all - suf - fi - cient mer - it Raise us to thy glo - rious throne.

Text: Charles Wesley, 1707–1788
Tune: W. Walker, Southern Harmony, 1835

9

Hark, the glad sound!

1 Hark, the glad sound! The Sav - ior comes, The Sav - ior
2 He comes the pris - 'ners to re - lease, In Sa - tan's
3 He comes the bro - ken heart to bind, The bleed - ing
4 Our glad ho - san - nas, Prince of Peace, Your wel - come

prom - ised long; Let ev - 'ry heart pre -
bond - age held. The gates of brass be -
soul to cure, And with the trea - sures
shall pro - claim, And heav'n's e - ter - nal

pare a throne And ev - 'ry voice a song.
fore him burst, The i - ron fet - ters yield.
of his grace To en - rich the hum - ble poor.
arch - es ring With your be - lov - ed name.

Text: Philip Doddridge, 1702-1751
Tune: attr. Thomas Haweis, 1734-1820

Oh, come, oh, come, Emmanuel

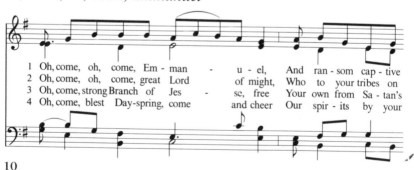

1 Oh, come, oh, come, Em - man - u - el, And ran - som cap - tive
2 Oh, come, oh, come, great Lord of might, Who to your tribes on
3 Oh, come, strong Branch of Jes - se, free Your own from Sa - tan's
4 Oh, come, blest Day-spring, come and cheer Our spir - its by your

10

Is - ra - el, That mourns in lone - ly ex - ile here
Si - nai's height In an - cient times once gave the law
tyr - an - ny; From depths of hell your peo - ple save
ad - vent here; Dis - perse the gloom - y clouds of night,

Un - til the Son of God ap - pear.
In cloud, and maj - es - ty, and awe.
And give them vic - t'ry o'er the grave. Re-joice! Re-joice!
And death's dark shad - ows put to flight.

Refrain

Em - man - u - el Shall come to you, O Is - ra - el.

5 Oh, come, O Key of David, come,
   And open wide our heav'nly home;
   Make safe the way that leads on high,
   And close the path to misery. *Refrain*

Text: Psalteriolum Cantionum Catholicarum, *Köln, 1710; tr. John M. Neale, 1818–1866, alt.*
Tune: French processional, 15th cent.

Wake, awake, for night is flying

1 Wake, a - wake, for night is fly - ing, The watch-men on the heights are cry - ing; A - wake, Je - ru - sa - lem, at last.

2 Zi - on hears the watch-men sing - ing, And in her heart new joy is spring - ing. She wakes, she ris - es from her gloom,

3 Now let all the heav'ns a - dore you, And saints and an - gels sing be - fore you. The harps and cym - bals all u - nite.

Mid - night hears the wel - come voic - es, And at the thrill - ing cry re - joic - es: "Come forth, you maid - ens! Night is past.

For her Lord comes down all - glo - rious, The strong in grace, in truth vic - to - rious. Her star is ris'n; her light is come.

Of one pearl each shin - ing por - tal, Where, dwell - ing with the choir im - mor - tal, We gath - er round your daz - zling light.

The bride-groom comes! A - wake; Your lamps with glad - ness take!"
Oh, come, you Bless - ed One, Lord Je - sus, God's own Son.
No eye has seen, no ear Has yet been trained to hear.

Al - le - lu - ia! Pre - pare your-selves to meet the
Sing ho - san - na! We go un - til the halls we
What joy is ours! Cre - scen - dos rise; your halls re -

Lord, Whose light has stirred the wait - ing guard.
view Where you have bid us dine with you.
sound; Ho - san - nas blend in cos - mic sound.

Text: Philipp Nicolai, 1556–1608; tr. Catherine Winkworth, 1829–1878, alt.
Tune: Philipp Nicolai, 1556–1608

Making an Advent Wreath

Use one of the suggestions given on the pages that follow to make an Advent wreath for use in your home.

Note: For each of the wreaths suggested, natural or artificial evergreens can be used. If using natural evergreens, never leave the candles burning unattended and replace the candles before they burn to less than six inches. Fire-retardant specifically for use with evergreen materials can be purchased. Otherwise, artificial silk or plastic evergreens can be used to make a wreath.

13

Styrofoam Wreath

Purchase a Styrofoam ring from a craft store. These come in a number of sizes, so choose one that is appropriate for your use. Purchase a length of ribbon approximately the same width and diameter as the outside ring, then glue or pin it around the outside base of the wreath. Place four candles of your choice evenly in the ring, pushing them down into the Styrofoam. If the candles tend to tip, remove them and put a small piece of clay of dab of glue from a hot-glue gun in the hole. Then replace the candles. Arrange evergreens around the candles, perhaps adding bows or decorations that represent Advent to the wreath.

Grapevine or Straw Wreath

Grapevine or straw wreaths can also be purchased from a craft store for use as an Advent wreath. Or, you may want to make a grapevine wreath yourself, using grapevines, if they are available, or another thin, pliable branch—such as that of a honeysuckle bush or birch tree. Strip any remaining leaves from the branches, then twist them together and form a circle. Once you have obtained the desired thickness, soak the wreath in warm water for 20 minutes, then reshape the circle if necessary.

Wire the candles to the wreath first, then add evergreens to hide the wiring. Wrap a length of gold or silver cording through the wreath and add other decorative items that symbolize the season of Advent.

Advent Yule Log

The Yule log is a Scandinavian tradition on the order of the Advent wreath, which can be adapted and used throughout the Advent season. Some families choose to save their Yule log for use in other years, while others burn it in the fireplace on Christmas Day to symbolize the light Jesus brought into the world.

To make an Advent Yule log, obtain a log that is approximately five to seven inches in diameter and is fairly clean, without an excess of moss or loose bark. Cut the log to a length of 20 inches. Flatten one side of the log so that it will not roll while in use. Drill four holes five inches apart along the top of the log. You may want to purchase the candles for the wreath before drilling the holes to ensure that the holes are drilled to the correct size. Then place the candles in the holes, using a small piece of clay or a dab of glue from a hot-glue gun in the bottom of the hole to hold them securely. Place a few evergreens along the top of the log and around the candles. Add a few pine cones, ribbon, or other decorations to complete the log.

Individual Advent Wreaths

Make individual Advent wreaths for classes, children, or family members. Cut a log that is approximately five to six inches in diameter into rounds two inches thick.

Lay the rounds flat and drill four holes evenly spaced around the perimeter of each round. Fit small candles into the holes, securing them with glue or clay. Allow individuals to decorate their own wreaths with real or artificial greens and other decorations.

ISBN-13: 978-0-8066-2375-7
ISBN-10: 0-8066-2375-6

9 780806 623757   9 0 0 0 0

AUGSBURG PUBLISHING HOUSE

Augsburg Fortress
www.augsburgfortress.org
10-23756